NO WORRIES

HOW TURNING WORRY INTO PRAYER CHANGED MY LIFE

RYAN BUNBURY

Revision Note to Reader:

On page 7 in the second paragraph of the Introduction, please replace *Mediate* with the word *Meditate*. The Scripture quoted should properly read: "Study this Book of Instruction continually. *Meditate* on it day and night so you will be sure to obey everything written in it. Only then will you prosper and succeed in all you do" (Joshua 1:8 NLT, emphasis added).

....

This Book is Saving Lives!
The proceeds of this book go toward generously
supporting Convoy of Hope, a faith-based, humanitarian
organization that provides food, water, emergency supplies
and agricultural know-how to help free people from
poverty, disease, and hunger. Convoy has unleashed hope
to more than one hundred million people throughout the
world, and your support will help save even more lives.

....

ISBN: 978-1-95756-605-4

Cover and Interior Design by Scot McDonald

LCCN:

Printed in the United States of America
1 2 3 4 5 6 7 8 9 10 Printing/Year 27 26 25 24 23

This book is dedicated to
Jesus and His Church; Linaya, Bryce, Gavin, and
Lilly; my family and friends; and all who have
encouraged me in my journey as an author. You
are all very much loved and appreciated.

Don't fret or worry. Instead of worrying, pray. Let petitions and praises shape your worries into prayers, letting God know your concerns. Before you know it, a sense of God's wholeness, everything coming together for good, will come and settle you down. It's wonderful what happens when Christ displaces worry at the center of your life.
—*Paul the Apostle, Philippians 4:6–7*

Contents

Introduction

Does what we think about *really* affect our overall health and well-being? In a weary world full of hopelessness, joylessness, and a whole lot of unhappy people, the Bible encourages, "Oh, the joys of those who ... delight in the law of the LORD, *meditating* on it day and night" (Psalm 1:1-2 NLT, emphasis added). Martin Laird, author of *Into the Silent Land: A Guide to the Christian Practice of Contemplation* said, "We are built for contemplation." If we truly are designed as contemplative creatures, perhaps meditating on the precepts our patriarchs meditated on and succeeded with is the prime practice and key toward finding inner peace in an anxious and worry-sick world. After all, the Bible has proven to be the world's best-selling book of all time and is filled with simple meditative practices and practical techniques for successful living that scientifically work.

The word *meditation* closely resembles the root meaning of the word *medication*. It makes perfect sense why the Lord prescribes, "Study this Book of Instruction continually. *Mediate* on it day and night so you will be sure to obey everything written in it. Only then will you prosper and succeed in all you do" (Joshua 1:8 NLT, emphasis added). It is right to deduce that sincere and systematic *meditation* on God's Word, the Bible, acts as an effective *medication* for the mind, body, and soul.

Living with type 1 diabetes has required me to follow an insulin prescription four to five times per day. The medication I faithfully take works favorably by keeping my body's blood glucose levels balanced, healthy, and whole. In the same way, living through the unprecedented times of the COVID-19 pandemic, economic uncertainty, and proliferated racial tension and turmoil has required me to call on Jesus and *meditate* on His Word like my life depends on it ... because it does. Spending time alone with Jesus every day, meditating on the Scripture and turning my worry into prayer, has not only helped me overcome my greatest challenges but undeniably brought my life hope, joy, peace, and certainly cerebral balance, health, and wholeness.

A Thirty-Day Worry-Free Prayer Challenge

I call my daily prayer and Bible study times with the Lord my *Coffee Time with Jesus*. I am continually learning to turn my worry into prayer in these most important times and have written this thirty-day worry-free challenge as an overflow from these transformative experiences. The theologized thoughts are pragmatically written as everyday life skills that I have learned and long to share with all my family and friends—*meditations* you, too, can benefit from.

Like an effective *medication*, this daily devotional is full of biblical *meditations* that have proven to encourage health, unleash hope, and inspire faith in hearts and minds. Dear reader, from my Seattle home to yours, I invite you to pull up a chair with Jesus and turn your worry into prayer.

Note to the Reader: Along with the daily contemplative readings, take the following prayer prescription three times per day for the next thirty days. Increase your prayer dosage if anxiety, fear, or worry symptoms persist. Furthermore, I have included a subsequent prayer that I personally prayed during my thirty-day challenge. I humbly submit my

Our Father which art in heaven, Hallowed be thy name. Thy kingdom come, Thy will be done in earth, as it is in heaven. Give us this day our daily bread. And forgive us our debts, as we forgive our debtors. And lead us not into temptation, but deliver us from evil: For thine is the kingdom, and the power, and the glory, for ever. Amen.

—*Jesus' Prayer Prescription (Matthew 6:9–13 KJV)*

testimony and story to you and offer my changed life and experience as observable evidence that prayer *really* works.

··

My Thirty-Day Worry-Free Turnaround Prayer

Jesus, with Your help, I am now emptying my mind of *all* anxiety, *all* fear, *all* sense of worry and insecurity. You prayerfully encourage me, "in prayer, believe . . . and it will be yours" (Mark 11:24 NIV). I believe in You and Your perfect Word. I actively say it three times: I believe. I believe. I believe. Jesus, I believe You are helping me to fill my mind with positive faith thoughts of fulfilled safety, strength, security, health, wholeness, hope, and happiness. My life is an everyday adventure with You, Lord, and I am enjoying Your unmerited favor and blessing. All inferiority is now leaving my mind, and Your unending hope, joy, and peace are now filling my life to overflowing. I love that I am Your child. I am confident You love me, and I know You are well pleased with me. In Jesus' name, amen.

Are You Listening?

"Are you listening to me? Really listening?"
—Jesus, Matthew 11:15

Have you ever had a hard time listening and *really* hearing what was being said? Perhaps you, like most people, are super busy and rushed a lot of the time.

Not too long ago, I entered my Seattle athletic club locker room after a workout only to see my personal locker had been blocked by a congregated group of sweaty men speedily getting ready. As I often do, I jokingly remarked with the guys, "Wow! It looks like another *traffic jam* in here today." I will never forget the disgruntled man who looked up at me with an obviously offended expression on his face. Fuming with anger he forcefully demanded, "Did you just call me *Jackie Chan*?!" With my indignant friend's nationality being the same as my wife's, and there being no sense of prejudice in my heart, I gently answered, "Sir, I made a rhetorical statement. The last thing I would ever want to do is intentionally offend anyone." I humbly reiterated, "Sir, it looks like another *traffic jam* in here, not you look like *Jackie Chan*."

In the same way, how often do you and I hear *Jackie Chan* stereotypes and offenses when anxiously in a *traffic jam*? In a busy world of schedules, to-do lists, and plenty of offenses, it is easy to not *really* listen. Dear reader, I have found God desires to get our attention because He deeply longs for relationship with us. He speaks with us and articulates His love through the Bible, books, friends, family, neighbors, coworkers, leaders, and, yes, even people in the gym locker room. The truth is, He is always speaking, and we are not always listening.

It is far too easy for us to end up feeling frustrated on the daily, looking for joy and peace but missing out because of our misunderstandings and lack of *really* listening to how Jesus is encouraging us and speaking hope. Here's the lesson: when we do not slow down long enough to listen to Jesus, we will ultimately be left feeling frustrated, undone, and completely unfulfilled.

If there is one thing I know full well, God has a good plan that He wants us to experience and live out. It includes love, joy, peace, patience, kindness, goodness, faithfulness, gentleness, and self-control. And, by the way, Jesus promises abundance of laughter and well-being.

> *Hearing God's voice is as simple as listening to that inner sensing inside your heart and soul and consciously paying attention to His still small voice deep inside you. It's a knowing in your "knower."*

But it is hard to hear all He is articulating when we are too busy living in a locker room of worry. If we are too busy thinking, talking, and doing, we are probably not *really* listening. Real talk . . . if you are offended by something someone has said to you, it's probably time to stop, drop, and pray. *"Are you listening to me? Really listening?"*

Is Jesus challenging you to be slow to speak and quick to listen (see James 1:19)? Be encouraged, hearing God is not some super-spiritual algorithm one has to learn. Hearing God is as simple as a personal encounter with the Spirit of Jesus. The ancient Jewish followers of God show evidence of *really* hearing Him. In the same way, "Your own ears will hear him. Right behind you a voice will say, 'This is the way you should go,' whether to the right or to the left" (Isaiah 30:21 NLT).

Let's take a few minutes now for some much-needed meditative quiet time and listening prayer with Jesus. You will know when you have heard Him. Begin by honestly telling Him all that is on your mind and in your heart. Turn your worry into prayer, and then take a few remaining minutes to *really* listen. Jesus is extending a personal prayer invitation to you now by asking, *"Are you listening to me? Really listening?"*

Turn Your Worry into Prayer

Dear Jesus, I believe You have a great plan for my life. I am truly sorry for busily squeezing You out and not listening because I've been preoccupied with my schedule and to-do list. My heart is open to Your Word now, and I am *really* listening. I trust You will help me to know and sense Your voice more clearly. I am turning to You now and turning my worry into prayer. I want nothing more than to want what You want me to want. Please help. In Jesus' name, amen.

Keep At It

*Depend on GOD and keep at it because in the
LORD GOD you have a sure thing.*
—*Isaiah 26:4*

Have you ever been stuck in the middle of something that seemingly was too difficult to overcome? It is easy to become bogged down with health challenges, financial issues, relationship heartache, and job conflicts.

The year 2018 was undoubtedly one of my most challenging years ever lived. Living in daily chronic physical ailment with type 1 diabetes, experiencing times of tension within relationships, all while having gone through almost a full year of unemployment gave me consciousness of need and provided me opportunity to get help from someone else besides myself. Who do you depend on for surety with your health and the next steps forward? Who do you turn to for unloading all your financial anxieties, fears, and worries? That Someone and Security for me has been the One and Only Jesus.

I 100 percent believe a relationship with Jesus gives everyone living in despair a renewed sense of hope. In my case, seeing my broken life put back together by the Lord was all the evidence I needed to believe Jesus is the answer.

Jesus has repeatedly helped me through every setback and sequence of unfortunate happenings I have experienced. He has been my source of strength to put one foot in front of the other when I have felt like giving up, to tenaciously *keep at it*. When I've felt like quitting, Isaiah's encouraging *keep at it* Scripture promises hope and has kept me going in the Lord, day by day, moment by moment.

Dear reader, whatever you are facing today, depend on God for the best possible outcome. Whatever you have been hoping for, prayerfully *keep at it*. Whatever you do, don't quit or give up on your dreams and aspirations because, like I did, you will find observable evidence in the Lord Jesus Christ that you have a sure thing—a hopeful future. Be encouraged, you can do all things through relationship with Jesus, Who promises to give you all the strength you will need to tenaciously *keep at it* (see Philippians 4:13).

....

Turn Your Worry into Prayer

Lord Jesus, thank You that I can wholeheartedly depend on You. I appreciate You giving me the supernatural power to *keep at it*. If there is one thing I know full well, I have a sure thing in You. You are my strength, my energy, my everything. Please lead me today in my thoughts, words, and actions to confidently and courageously *keep at it*. I am turning to You now and turning my worry into prayer. I trust You are sovereign, believe Your Word is true, and prayerfully acknowledge Your presence as the evidence of my surety. In Jesus' name, amen.

Don't Panic!

"Don't panic. I'm right here to help you."
—The Lord, Isaiah 41:13

Have you ever been in a situation that was completely out of your control? Has something or someone ever caused anxiety and stress to rise within you?

One rainy Seattle afternoon, I was on my way to the Sea-Tac Airport to catch a very important flight for a speaking engagement. Understand, this trip was nonnegotiable and vitally important for me because I had been unemployed, and it was an interview for a job opportunity that I *really* needed. Unfortunately, as it often does in a metropolis of over four million people, everything came to a screeching halt due to a major big rig accident on I-5. This resulted in the commute not taking the hour it usually would but nearly three hours for me to drive just twenty-five miles. This ultimately resulted in me missing my flight—big bummer.

As you can imagine, my negative reactions and inner mind movies to all the accident traffic and lookie-loo drivers led to an even greater pileup inside me of anxiety, fear, and worry. Negative emotions increased as I ruminated on lies the enemy whispered in my head: "You aren't going to make your interview. You're such a failure. Everyone is going to think you are unreliable. Ryan, you are nothing short of disappointing."

Then I had a life-changing thought as I suddenly sensed a scriptural promise from the Spirit of Jesus in my heart. *"Don't panic.*

I'm right here to help you." In response, I prayed my worry back to the Lord: "I admit to feeling overwhelmed with worry, but I prayerfully choose to trust that You will always be on time and help do for me everything I cannot do for myself." Jesus changed my perspective for the better by helping me with a prayer prescription.

Through honest confession this prayerful process resulted in a positive overflow of observable evidence in my life: laughter, joy, peace, happiness, and well-being.

I would like to say my negotiating skills were what caused the airline agent to reissue a supposedly "nonrefundable," "nontransferable" ticket, but I know better. It was Jesus who helped me. He made a way where there seemed to be no way. The Spirit of Jesus helped me pray instead of panic. He was with me all the way. Moreover, it was not so much that I received a new flight to a job offer (that I ended up turning down), as it was knowing the Lord Jesus Christ was with me all along the adventurous journey.

In the same way an optometrist prescribes new glasses to help you see clearly again, trusting Dr. Jesus with your blurry worry and turning panic into prayer will help you stop stressing and start seeing your situation clearly again with a brand-new outlook.

Dear reader, be encouraged, Jesus is with you now to help you with whatever challenges you are facing. Traffic and all, *don't panic,* you are in good hands and not alone. Jesus is with you and promises to help get you where you need to go. Here is the question: will you trust Jesus enough to give Him your fear and worry in exchange for His joy and peace?

Turn Your Worry into Prayer

Dear Jesus, thank You that You are right here and with me to help me. I'm sorry for being reactionary at times by anxiously panicking. Please help me to cast all my cares on You and to wholly trust that You will work everything out in my favor. I am turning to You now and turning my worry into prayer. In exchange for my piled-up anxiety, panic-filled fear, and blurry worry, please fill my mind with Your prescribed hope, joy, peace, happiness, and well-being. In Jesus' name, amen.

Bless Your Enemies

*Bless your enemies; no cursing
under your breath.*
—Romans 12:14

Do you know the bitter feelings of being hurt or betrayed by someone? Is there an enemy in your life, someone who actively opposes you, who has severely wronged you in one way or another and caused offense?

There is nothing more difficult than facing hurt feelings and negative emotions experienced from hostile harassment and ill treatment from others. Trust me when I say that I know what I'm talking about regarding offense. Beyond my MA in Leadership, I have gained a "degree" of life experience from the inner-city streets of Seattle. I understand wrongdoing—I've been misunderstood, profiled, threatened, cursed at, physically pushed, robbed, ridiculed, hated, falsely accused, and unjustly laid off. I've also learned forging forward is 100 percent possible by taking all unforgiveness to Jesus and asking Him for help to forgive. Truth be told, He's remarkably great with helping this way.

Jesus prescribes a bittersweet medicine when you find yourself sick of being offended, angry, or resentful: "Bless your enemies."

When what you face becomes overwhelming, unbearable, seemingly hopeless, and insurmountably unchangeable, dear reader, "don't quit in hard times; pray all the harder" (Romans 12:12). One of the best ways to find peace again is to *bless your enemies* by praying for them. Forgiveness 101: Refuse to bless publicly yet curse privately under your breath. Prayer helps with this. Turn your hurt feelings and bitterness into honest prayers to Jesus. What emotionally claims to be *over* you really is *under* you through overcoming prayer. Keep your prayers simple, short, and honest. Always keep your prayers going. Take it from me, if you keep on praying, your feelings will eventually catch up with your will. Remember, if God allowed you to experience it, He will faithfully lead you through it.

Your victory and promised peace lie not with insisting on getting even through retribution or by taking revenge but in prayerfully overcoming the ill will done you—*bless your enemies*. Be encouraged, forgiveness is not letting go of the memories but letting go of the hate while trusting God enough to surrender all your hurts and offenses into His sovereign hands. The truth is, the stronger you hold on to unforgiveness, the weaker you ultimately become. I've learned by choosing to *bless your enemies,* by forgiving and praying over them, you will, in time, feel God's healing, experience Jesus' strength, and be changed with the curative Spirit of Jesus' love— finding happiness and well-being deep within your soul.

Is praying Jesus' love over your enemies an easy thing to do? No. Is it essential for you to experience peace within? Yes—*bless your enemies.*

....

Turn Your Worry into Prayer

Dear Jesus, thank You for forgiving me. I'm sorry for all my offenses and sins. Please help me to forgive those who have deeply offended me. Help me to soften my heart and harden my feet (not the other way around) and genuinely bless my enemies in my thoughts, words, and actions. I will overcome the evil things done to me by doing good to those who despise me. Confident in Your love and empowered with Your Spirit's joy and peace, I align my life and will with Your way of doing things. I am turning to You now and turning my worry into prayer. I both hear and heed Your prescribed words of *bless your enemies.* In Jesus' name, amen.

Trust and Pray

*Trust in the LORD with all your heart and lean not on
your own understanding; in all your ways submit to
him, and he will make your paths straight.*
—Proverbs 3:5-6 NIV

Do you ever find it challenging to trust the Lord enough to slow down and pray?

I distinctly remember learning to *trust and pray* growing up because of my parents. It was during my formative years when my mom would make my favorite breakfast while leading me in scriptural meditation, memorization, and prayer. As an adolescent, I remember thinking this routine a little inconvenient while I was trying to consume my scrambled eggs and toast. But because it was my mom, I could *trust and pray.*

Now, as an adult who enjoys his scrambled eggs on top of the Farmer's Hash Bowl at my all-time favorite Seattle breakfast spot, Portage Bay Cafe, I am helping others discover these nourishing truths and the power of meditative prayer. I am deeply grateful for this theological framework that my mom helped me fortify in my contemplative mind and longing heart.

In the face of the unprecedented and uncertain times of the COVID-19 pandemic, I recall using this timeless truth for initiating a simple way for my family to trust and pray. I found a container and wrote on the front of it one of my favorite Jesus quotes from Matthew 19:26: "With God all things are possible" (NIV). I then asked everyone to personally write their greatest need, challenge, or problem down on paper and trust God enough to give it to Him in prayer. One by one, we put our troubles in the container and turned our worry into prayer. As a result, we have witnessed the evidence of physical, emotional, and relational healing, financial provision, comfort, joy, and peace among a myriad of other God-sized miracles. Wow—awesome! Praise the Lord— thank You, Jesus! Learning to *trust and pray* has completely changed the trajectory of my family.

Concurrent in thought, this fundamental discipline is very practical and easy enough for anyone to put into practice. Prayer always aligns the way we do things with the way God does things . . . which 100 percent works.

> *When we pray, we begin to trust God more; and when we trust God more, we begin to pray.*

Isaiah deduced, "When you pray, GOD will answer" (Isaiah 58:9). Jesus articulated, "Whatever you ask for in prayer, believe that you have received it, and it will be yours" (Mark 11:24 NIV). These are some of my all-time favorite ancient Scripture promises from God. Furthermore, William Temple, former Archbishop of Canterbury, once said, "When I pray, coincidences happen; when I don't, they don't." Whether it's physical, emotional, relational, or spiritual, learning to *trust and pray* not only means you will experience a series of "coincidences," but you will enjoy life so much more by living anxiety-free. Will you take a moment now to *trust and pray*?

Turn Your Worry into Prayer

Dear Jesus, thank You for Your promise to answer me when I pray. I'm sorry for not trusting You and praying more often. Please give me Your grace to relinquish all my anxiety, fear, and worry. I wholeheartedly believe that taking time today to *trust and pray* will result in my fullness of Your joy and peace. Your Word promises that I can have abundant life in You if I will only *trust and pray*. So, I pray all uncertainty and unknown things with full faith in You. I am turning my mind over to You right now and turning my worry into prayer. In Jesus' name, amen.

Faith in God

When it all seemed hopeless, Abraham
still had faith in God.
—Romans 4:18 CEV

Have you ever faced something that seemed completely hopeless? Not long ago my family was faced with the horrifying news that my dad had been diagnosed with stage 4 colon cancer. I cannot begin to adequately articulate or express how difficult this was for all of us. It was a long fight and, at times, terribly discouraging. We struggled watching him suffer. Can you relate to looking death in the face and feeling uncertain with what's next? Be encouraged, dear reader, when all seems hopeless, *faith in God* will make a way. With faithful support from friends and family, turning worry into prayer, and the miracle of modern-day medicine, God was gracious and marvelously healed my dad.

If you are facing a seemingly hopeless situation, despairing even of life, Scripture affirms that He is "the God who gives life to the dead and calls into being things that were not" (Romans 4:17 NIV). Against all odds, hope believes by having *faith in God*. The accuser will try to steal your laughter, kill your joy, and destroy your happiness and well-being. He will work overtime to try to distract your mind from believing in God by telling you lies like "You can't take it," "You won't make it," and "You are unable to do it; you may as well give up hope." Don't believe that cancer-like thinking; flip the script and have *faith in God*. With a confident expectation, believe something great will happen in your favor.

The Bible tells the story of how God promised Abraham he would be given a lot of descendants. This was seemingly hopeless, considering Abraham received this mind-bending promise when he was in his seventies. The biblical narrative goes on to describe a one-hundred-year-old Abraham (see Genesis 21:5), whose body was old and as good as dead. But Scripture observes the evidence of a living God Who was not done working in Abraham. How exactly? Ancient Abraham's timeworn wife became pregnant, and he became the father of Isaac and the ancestral father of the nations (see Romans 4:18). True story.

In the same way, even though things have not gone according to your plan or timeline, God still has the master blueprint and is not finished working on your behalf. If it's undone, God's not done. If the Lord Jesus Christ has not yet answered your prayers like you thought He would, and things have not turned out the way you had hoped they would, remember God is still in control and will answer at the right time in the right way.

In the same way chemotherapy acts as the healing agent by killing cancerous cells, there is no better antidote to worry than prayer therapy. Faith in God is a hope-filled medicine that will bring healing to your anxious mind and worry sickness.

When all seems hopeless, consider Abraham and remember my family. In other words, have *faith in God*. Jesus ultimately promises eternal life for all who hope and believe in Him. If you will take time today to put your *faith in God* and prayerfully give Him your anxious thoughts and fearful uncertainty, He has promised to provide you with all you will ever need. Do you have any uncertainty about your future? Be encouraged to turn your worry into prayer because believing prayer works.

When it all seems hopeless, like it did for Abraham, you can still have *faith in God*. Here is the lesson to think about: if our forefathers articulated that prayer works, and the ancient Scriptures give us observable evidence as such, why not push the pause button on the despairing hopelessness and discouragement surrounding your cancer-like worry and give prayer a try?

Turn Your Worry into Prayer

Dear Jesus, thank You for Your saving and healing power. You are an awesome God Whose promises are true. In hope, I believe You will give life to every dead area in my mind, body, and spirit. In You, and with a faith-filled heart, I am calling things that are not as though they were. Against all odds, when things seem impossible, I will have *faith in God*. I am turning to You now and turning my worry into prayer. Please help me overcome. In Jesus' name, amen.

Get Me Out of This

"My Father, if there is any way, get me out of this. But
please, not what I want. You, what do you want?"
—*Jesus, Matthew 26:39*

Have you ever found yourself stuck in the middle of an overwhelming situation and thought, *Get me out of this?* If you have ever experienced insurmountable distress, then you can most definitely relate to the emotional exhaustion Jesus felt when He articulated this prayer.

The Scripture narrates, not once or twice but three times, that Jesus prayed His uneasiness back to God. Be encouraged, you are not alone in your consciousness of distress. Jesus prayed under immense pressure too. When facing times of sorrow and suffering, feeling the weight of the cross in His Spirit long before His body felt the actual brutality and inhumane elaborations of the crucifixion, Jesus showed us where He found His strength to carry on. We, too, have access to the One Who promises to empower through His good graces.

In one of the more difficult seasons I faced, I must confess my utter disappointment as I miserably worked a ministry job that sucked all the life out of me and sent me home weary every night, feeling undervalued, misunderstood, and dejected. The people and team you are surrounded with can either make or break your quiet confidence. It was here, in a dark and dismal state of lonely affairs, with a lack of support and care, where Jesus reminded me, "Ryan, I, too, have prayed, '*Get me out of this.*'"

What suffering, hardship, and pain have you faced with a languishing strain? Though our circumstances do not physically crucify us, like with Jesus, the distressing feelings are relatable and real enough where they leave the heart feeling sorrowfully nailed with strain and maimed with pain. In the face of opposition, be encouraged to pray all your worry back to the Lord and "cast all your anxiety on him because he cares for you" (1 Peter 5:7 NIV). If there is one thing I know full well, following Jesus' model of prayer changes everything—quite literally, *every* thing. Moreover, Jesus exemplified prayer as simply being conversation with God that transforms fear into faith, sorrow into strength, pain into provision, and death into life. Circumstances may seemingly prove unbearable, but prayer will always unleash God's supernatural power to do the impossible in your life, starting in your mind.

> *By aligning your will with His and echoing Jesus' prayer—"My Father, if there is any way, get me out of this. But please, not what I want. You, what do you want?"—you exchange your overpowering problems with His overwhelming peace. Prayer works.*

Dear reader, through prayer you will soon see that God has a plan that involves you overcoming—coming over everything that proves against you. Perhaps the best thing to do right now is to briefly pause and take a moment to converse with Jesus with a genuine, heartfelt prayer.

Turn Your Worry into Prayer

Dear Jesus, thank You that You know everything I am going through in my life right now. I am sorry for not coming to You sooner with my honest prayer. Please help me to trust You by surrendering my will and following Your way. I want nothing more than to want what You want me to want. Like You did on that bitter dark night in the Garden of Gethsemane, I am turning to You now and turning my worry into prayer. In the face of every difficulty that I want out of, I thank You for helping me overcome my darkest of times victoriously and with a peace that passes all my understanding. "Thy will be done." In Jesus' name, amen.

Throw Off

Let us throw off everything that hinders
and the sin that so easily entangles.
—Hebrews 12:1 NIV

Have you ever accidently started driving your car with the emergency brake still engaged? I admit that I have done this more than once, usually because I was distracted. Nonetheless, when I recognized my mistake, and that my vehicle was being held back and hindered from its fullest driving potential, I immediately *threw off* the brake. In the same way, if there is something you consciously can recognize as a hindrance, now is the time to *throw off* the entanglement. Is there anything in your life that is acting like a brake and holding you back from reaching your fullest potential in Christ Jesus?

I have found being hurt relationally can cause some of the greatest pain and, if not taken to the Lord in prayer, can act as a brake of bitterness that holds you back from living an abundantly happy life. Additionally, habitual unhealthy thought patterns that consist of comparing the worst of yourself with the best of others only results in a brake of negativity. This, too, will hold you back. Fatalistic thinking, deep discouragement, and debilitating regret are all resultant ruminations that hinder and entangle an anxious mind stuck and in need of emotional healing and freedom. Furthermore, staying hung up with feelings of guilt, grief, or shame from something you did or didn't do in the past is a brake of condemnation that will undoubtedly hold you back. These are a few examples of hindrances and interruptions that, for a momentary season of prayerlessness, became my *breaking* point and kept me from experiencing true freedom and breakthrough in Christ Jesus.

The Bible encourages us to *throw off* everything that holds us back and enslaves us. If you desire joy and peace, happiness and well-being, today is the perfect day and opportunity to throw aside all bitter hurts, to throw out all self-imposed inferiority and comparison-ridden thoughts, and to *throw off* every encumbrance that so easily entangles, hinders, and holds you back from a fulfilled life of freedom in Christ Jesus. If it's not helping you to find abundant life, it's hindering and holding you back. If you can acknowledge being held back, biblical wisdom advises you to *throw off* the brake and break free.

> *Jesus wants nothing more than for you to be completely carefree in His care. So, throw off all the bad breaks that have hindered your freedom, confess your consciousness of all sin that has entangled and held you back, and move forward in Christ by turning your worry into prayer.*

Here is the lesson: prayerfully confessing your offenses, hurt feelings, bad habits, negative thinking, and hang-ups to Jesus is like suddenly experiencing the feeling of freedom after releasing the emergency brake. As you *throw off* all hindrances, you will experience His breakthrough power that will drive your potential and life forward to places you have never dreamed possible.

Turn Your Worry into Prayer

Dear Jesus, thank You for Your saving help. I'm sorry for sinning in my thoughts, words, and actions. Please help me to *throw off* every encumbrance that hinders my potential and holds me back from Your joy and peace. I am turning to You now and turning my worry into prayer by asking for Your strength and enduring power to overcome and never quit. I consciously choose to trust You and the intellect of Your Spirit deep within me. In Jesus' name, amen.

God Cares for You

God cares for you, so turn all your worries over to him.
—1 Peter 5:7 CEV

Have you ever faced a situation that was overwhelming and felt unbearable? Perhaps you are stuck in the middle of a mess even now. When facing troubles, difficulties, or disappointments, anxiety tends to trail. Many of our personal problems, stressful worries, and everyday concerns can tend to be financially related and economic in nature, whether our anxiety is connected to endless debt, taxes, or ever-increasing health-care expenses.

Not long ago I was faced with an unfortunate season of unemployment. After eight long months, I still had a mortgage, bills, and a family to provide for. Additionally, my type 1 diabetes monthly prescriptions and doctor bills piled up. I was confronted with a major decision: do I live in faith or fear? I hate to admit it, but before I realized it, my life script had turned toxic and negative, full of worry. Fear seemed to relentlessly threaten: "Ryan, you are a failure and a disappointment at best. Look at you . . . Do you *really* think God cares for you?"

I confess that, like most of us, I wrestled with these thoughts for quite some time. Then, one morning, a faith-filled thought and prayer disrupted my hopelessness: "Ryan, *God cares for you*, so turn all your worries over to Him. He wants nothing more than to save you from all your greatest fears." I made a decision to live carefree by resting in His care. Simply put, I turned all my worry into prayer, and it 100 percent worked in my favor.

Prayer 101: When we pray, God will do for us that which we cannot do for ourselves. Ironically, Jesus used some of the same people in the organization that actively opposed me and laid me off to provide the necessary financial means that helped me and my family make it through the hardest of times. Every month when my doorbell rang with a check from a contributor, I was generously reminded, "Ryan, *God cares for you.*" Dear reader, if He can take care of me, He can take care of you. *God cares for you.* Whatever you are faced with today, let go of your anxiety, fear, and worry. Be encouraged, Jesus truly cares about every detail of your life, big and small.

He *really* wants to help you through your challenges and heartaches. God is undoubtedly more than enough, despite your shortages and setbacks. His promised loving-kindness, compassion, and care will make a way for you through the seemingly impossible. When you turn all your worries over to Jesus and wholeheartedly give your life to Him, He promises to save you and work in your favor (see Romans 10:13). Will you cast all your cares on Him, because *God cares for you?* You should know, the Lord redefined my unemployment as the worst-*best* season of life.

> *When my worst fears were recognized, my best faith was realized. So be encouraged, dear reader, in the same way Jesus used my mess to articulate His MESSage of hope, loving-kindness, compassion, and care, He will prove Himself to you too. God cares for you.*

All your hopes and needs, all your fears and dreams—entrust them all to Jesus. God lovingly cares for you, so prayerfully turn all your worry over to Him.

Turn Your Worry into Prayer

Dear Jesus, thank You that I can cast all my cares on You. I'm sorry for anxiously taking matters into my own hands. Please help me to prayerfully turn all my worries over to You. I give You all my hopes and needs, my fears and dreams today. Whatever I am faced with, I know You deeply care for me. I give my health, family, job, and finances to You and am trusting You for the optimal outcome. I am turning to You now and turning my worry into prayer. I surrender to Your will and choose to wholeheartedly trust Your perfect plan. In Jesus' name, amen.

I Can

I can do all things through Christ
who strengthens me.
—Philippians 4:13 NKJV

Can you believe that Paul the Apostle wrote these words in one of his most joyful epistles while he notably was stuck in a dark and dismal prison chamber? These ten words articulated from a first-century jail cell have forever changed my life. Perhaps you are currently locked inside of a prison-like challenge, a time of heart-wrenching grief or trauma that has proven to be deeply troublesome. Dear reader, be encouraged; if you understand what being surrounded by walls of difficulty feels like, you are not alone.

Confession from a man who wears a myriad of hats: as a husband, father, reverend, church board president, Rotarian, and community leader, I have, at times, wrestled with a great degree of anxiousness, stress, and worry while managing innumerable responsibilities. There are times when the burdens I bear leave me feeling trapped, like an imprisonment.

What are *your* prison-like walls? Prison walls can look a lot like being unjustly laid off and chained to unemployment; humiliated with bad breaks and false allegations; stuck with a burden of disappointment in between big dreams and a small budget; beaten down by never-ending criticisms and ever-increasing responsibilities; hospitalized and bedridden with a slew of health complications and bills to boot. Whether or not these examples resonate with you, I'm sure we all understand the pain of prison-like walls. But, dear reader, it does not have to end with worry.

Paul enunciated *where* we can find strength when depleted by our wearisome troubles. In our prison, we are given opportunities to either think "I can't" or believe *"I can."* When we face bad brakes, many of us despondently find ourselves tied down by the fatalistic words *"I can't."* We think, "I can't because I'm not able or skilled," or "I can't because I don't have enough talent or influence." But, through the supernatural strength of Christ Jesus, God came to set us free from the prison of inferiority and all the *"I can't do it"* negative thinking. With Jesus, you have what it takes and 100 percent *can* do it. Prayerfully allow these words to echo in the depths of your soul: *"I can!"* Repeat them again and again until you believe them.

In the same way Paul prayerfully articulated God's life-giving Word in his suffering, hardship, and trial, I have learned that by turning my worry into prayer and assenting, "I can in Christ," I, too, can experience Jesus' abundant joy, peace, happiness, and well-being, especially in the darkest of my difficulties.

Paul deduced that Christ gives us strength to face anything and everything with a can-do attitude. With Jesus, God's "super" meets our "natural"—*I can* do all things supernaturally through Christ. With Jesus, God's "extra" meets our "ordinary"—*I can* do all things extraordinarily through Christ. Through Christ Jesus, the new life script etched in the mind has become: *"I can* because I am well able and skilled." *"I can* because I now have the ability and superpower needed." *"I can* because I can do all things through Christ who strengthens me."

Regardless of what is currently going on around you and all the responsibilities you bear, you can be freed from the prison walls of "I can't" and live renewed in the hopeful promise, strength, and power of "*I can.*" Be encouraged and prayerfully believe: "*I can* do it." "*I can* take it." "*I can* make it." "Through Christ Jesus *I can!*"

Turn Your Worry into Prayer

Dear Jesus, thank You that with Christ Jesus I have what it takes to do all the things I need to do today. In every prison-like experience I am facing, You have promised to give me Your strength. I confess that at times I rely on my own intellect and strength. Please help me to surrender and trust You more. Please help me to rely less on myself and more on Your strength to see me through. I am turning to You now and turning my worry into prayer. In Jesus' name, amen.

Stay with God

Take heart. Don't quit . . . Stay with GOD.
—*Psalm 27:14*

How often do we ask ourselves the never-ceasing, mostly unanswerable question, "Why?" *Why* did my loved one have to pass away with that disease? *Why* do the innocent suffer inhumanely? *Why* am I going through this heart-wrenching pain . . . again? At some point we all want to know *why*—what's the *why?*

I have found there are some *why* questions in life that may never be answered or even understood. In the face of not knowing the *why*, there is a different question I have learned is worth exploring. It is the question that helps us prayerfully look up and move forward. The resolute question is this: "What's next?" *What's next?* helps articulate clarity of vision and is a sure way that moves you forward.

In one of my morning prayer times, I sensed this reflective question that has helped transform me by the renewing of my mind (see Romans 12:2): "What's next for you, Ryan? Will you confidently and courageously *stay with God* despite all the unknown *whys?*" A thought-provoking question, indeed, for me to ruminate on while sipping my Seattle French press coffee with Jesus.

The ancient Jewish writers obviously shared some of the same *why* questions when they faced worrisome times. Take the Psalmist David, for example, as one who understood opposition. "My God, my God, *why* have you forsaken me?" (Psalm 22:1 NIV, emphasis added). David also knew the benefits of keeping company with God amid his excruciating pain, extreme difficulties—like facing the giant Goliath—and unexplainable *whys*.

> *David could have stayed back with everyone else trying to answer "Why?" when Goliath defied God. Instead, he looked up, moved forward, and overcame his giant problem by prayerfully asking God, "What's next?".*

David's example emphatically encourages us all to *stay with God* when facing life's giant problems. David's undeserved, unearned success over his setbacks narrates that the giant challenges in front of us will never be bigger than the Most High God inside of us. The troubles you encounter can never overtake you when you *stay with God*. Depend on God and keep at it because in the Lord you have a sure thing. Staying with God means staying hopeful.

Jesus echoed David's words in Psalm 22:1 when He prayed from the cross, "My God, my God, *why* have you forsaken me?" (Mark 15:34 NIV, emphasis added). Hanging from a bloodied cross, Jesus showed us that every problem is an opportunity to find a solution; every solution is found in God; therefore, every problem is an opportunity to find God. Whether sickness, bodily pain, heartache, disillusionment, a bad relationship break, or financial turmoil, it is an opportunity to find resolution with the Lord.

In the same way I have decided to steadfastly believe for healing despite my type 1 diabetes diagnosis, you, too, can prayerfully turn your worry into faith-filled, giant-slaying overcoming prayer. Even in the face of death, Jesus stayed with God and prayed His way through His *why*. In the same way, today, take heart, don't quit, and *stay with God*. Be encouraged, dear reader; the greatness and power of His love is sure to be your source.

Turn Your Worry into Prayer

Dear Jesus, thank You for another day of opportunity. Like David, I am facing giant challenges and need Your help. I'm sorry for not trusting You more. I am turning to You now and turning my worry into prayer. Please help me take heart and not quit. I give You my heart and confess that I will confidently stay the course and *stay with God*. In Jesus' name, amen.

The God of Hope

May the God of hope fill you with all joy and peace as
you trust in him, so that you may overflow with hope by
the power of the Holy Spirit.
—Romans 15:13 NIV

On a scale of 1 to 10, are you a happy and hopeful person full of joy and peace? It can be frustrating not to totally be in touch with *why* your heart feels void of joy and peace, especially if you are known by others as a Christian and theoretically living an abundantly blessed life.

Money, power, sex, relationships, position, popularity, education, substance abuse, food medicating, social media obsessions, and self-righteous comparisons can never reconcile your deepest need to be satisfied with joy and peace within you. What all have you endlessly tried to fill the void with?

Paul the Apostle was one who profoundly knew joy and peace amid arduous circumstances. He pointed us toward Christ Jesus as the key. *The God of Hope* is the One and Only Who can truly satisfy your deepest

Men, women, boys, and girls who do not have the God of Hope's joy and peace in their hearts will vainly spend their entire lifetime trying to find it elsewhere. I can say this because I know what it feels like to have endlessly tried.

need for love. If there is one thing the Lord so desires, it is to satisfy the inmost desire of your heart. Think about it . . . Jesus could live anywhere in the entire universe and yet He chooses to live in your heart. The Lord longs to fill you with His joy and peace as you learn to trust in Him.

In a most difficult season of my life, I had experienced an immense amount of loss and was suffering borderline burnout and mental breakdown. As a depressed pastor who preached hope while wrestling with despair, I confess that I turned to food to medicate. Resultantly, my overeating didn't fill the void or give me peace within. On the contrary, medicating with food only gave me a supersized serving of self-consciousness and anxiety alongside fifty extra pounds of weight that would take me years to overcome— dangerously not good as a type 1 diabetic.

I distinctly remember the day when my endocrinologist concernedly showed me my out-of-balance diabetic blood glucose levels, terrible test results, and a negative prognosis—all subsequent conversations with my doctor, who repeatedly advised a lifestyle change. As a Jesus follower, I saw the deeper connection and knew this was, in fact, the Great Physician using my diabetic doctor to encourage a life-or-death turnaround in my life.

I have learned that anxiety, fear, and worry can cause prolific pain and, at the core, lead to destructive behavior. It's important for you to remember that the enemy of your soul wants nothing more than to steal your laughter, kill your joy, and destroy your happiness and well-being. But, dear reader, please know that *the God of Hope* has a name, and that name is Jesus. Jesus, *the God of Hope*, wants nothing more than to fill your heart with all joy and peace. In knowing Him, we are promised to abundantly know life, hope, joy, and peace.

We will truly know what all of this means when we trust enough to follow Him. We can know and be known by *the God of Hope* when we prayerfully find and follow Jesus. This is my turnaround story. If your heart feels hopelessly anxious, if you have unhappily tried a million little things, try praying. Turning your life around begins by turning your worry into prayer.

Turn Your Worry into Prayer

Dear Jesus, thank You for the hope I have in You. I am sorry for wondering and wandering, hopelessly searching for joy and peace in temporal things. Please help me to wholeheartedly trust in You. I am turning to You now and turning my worry into prayer. In my turnaround, please fill me with Your abundant hope. I choose You, *the God of Hope*, and trust only You for my utmost happiness and well-being. In Jesus' name, amen.

They Gave Me a Pulpit

Everything happening to me in this jail only serves to make Christ more accurately known, regardless of whether I live or die. They didn't shut me up; they gave me a pulpit!
—Philippians 1:20

Have you ever found yourself seemingly imprisoned by a bad break? Real talk . . . I have, repeatedly, with T1D (type 1 diabetes).

I was in my early twenties, a young goal-oriented pastor, tenaciously full of passion and drive, and I felt completely unstoppable . . . until I suddenly was. I remember feeling so sick that I thought I was going to die. I was extremely thirsty, dizzy, unable to think clearly, shaking, sweating, having difficulty speaking, losing coordination, and thinking I was going blind due to my blurred vision. Miraculously, I was somehow able to drive myself to the hospital to get help. The last thing I remember on the day I almost died in Las Vegas was arriving at the emergency room check-in and everything suddenly blacking out.

My blood glucose, or blood sugar, which is supposed to be at a healthy balance between 80 and 120 mg/dL, had dangerously spiked to well over 700 mg/dL. I had suddenly slipped into unconsciousness and found myself imprisoned by the terrible darkness of a diabetic coma. Close to twenty-four hours later I woke up to a room full of people who all had that concerned look on their faces that tells you something is *very* wrong. Hearing my doctor diagnose me with type 1 diabetes and being told the myriad of ways my life would never be the same woke me up to feeling worried sick. News like this will flood your mind with anxiety quicker than a Humalog KwikPen shot will fill your body with insulin.

If unfamiliar with the chronic illness, type 1 diabetes is an autoimmune disease where the body's insulin-producing beta cells in the pancreas have somehow been destroyed by the immune system. I have come to learn diabetes is a disease that does not want to be controlled. In the same way, worry will do everything to imprison you and destroy your happiness and well-being. Like the callouses my skin has formed from me having to administer four-plus shots every day, diabetes has proved to be a prison that has toughened me up in many ways. If you are someone living with a debilitating disease, be encouraged, there is hope. My story offers observable evidence that your hardship does not have to only be a prison; it can also serve as a pulpit.

Paul the Apostle articulated his prison as an opportunity to share the hope of Jesus with those who were also in the same dark, dingy dungeon—*they gave me a pulpit!* A pulpit is something that can be used to share the Good News and Gospel message of Jesus' hope. Dear reader, it's not the event but the meaning we give to the event that ultimately determines its impact. Therefore, diabetes has not shut me up but has 100 percent given me a pulpit to proclaim the hope of Jesus. In the same way, could the current sickness, pain, debt, disease, doubt, anxiety, fear, or worry you are currently chained to be used as a pulpit to proclaim the hope-filled message of Jesus?

No matter the darkness you have experienced, nothing and no

> *When they diagnosed me with type 1 diabetes, they didn't shut me up; they gave me a pulpit! In the same way, your bad break doesn't have to shut you up in a prison of discouragement; it can be used for proclaiming hope and helping people find and follow the Great Physician—Jesus.*

one can shut you up! Yes, a bad break is an undesired setback, but your story does not have to end that way.

As a community leader, I have been able to articulate my turnaround story in many creative ways. Whether it's the *Jesus Loves Seattle* Homeless Hope Bags stories I've shared with the fire chief at Rotary or the stories of hope I've shared with countless Seattle neighbors in our church's dog bark, *they gave me a pulpit!* Did you catch that? We named the dog park at Calvary our dog *bark*. The dog bark is one of our *Jesus Loves Seattle* outreaches for our neighbors and their fur babies. I have personally helped people find and follow Jesus in the dog bark by simply sharing my story. In the same way, dear reader, your happenings can serve as a pulpit to proclaim the life-changing hope of Jesus.

....

Turn Your Worry into Prayer

Dear Jesus, thank You for helping me when I am imprisoned with worry. I am sorry for anxiously staying chained to my cares and concerns when You have offered to free me from them all. I am turning to You now and turning my worry into prayer. Please help me to use my situation as a pulpit. I really want to experience Your provision and share Your love more with others. May my life be observable evidence that You really and truly are the Great Physician and offer hope for all in despair. In Jesus' name, amen.

When You Are Weak

"My gift of undeserved grace is all you need.
My power is strongest when you are weak."
—*Jesus, 2 Corinthians 12:9* CEV

What troubles, hardships, and difficulties have caused you to feel weak and weary? Here is something to think about: a seeming defeat can be a setup for a God-sized victory. Be encouraged, *when you are weak*, the Bible reminds us that God gives life to dead places and calls things that are not as though they were (see Romans 4:17). When enduring tough times, what would happen if you saw it as a setup to become stronger by growing more resilient in your faith?

Allow me to illustrate the point by articulating it this way: I absolutely love-hate the gym. There has never been a workout I have lovingly longed to do. Concurrently, there has never been a workout I have hatefully regretted. I like to say it this way: *a healthy heart means a healthy start . . . every single day.* Fitness is one of my nonnegotiable disciplines and a big part of my daily routine.

Once, while working out early in the morning with my physical fitness trainer, I started complaining, "I feel weak and defeated today. I'm tired, and this is *really* hard!" My laughing friend and trainer replied, "LOL! That's the whole point of being here! Just trust me, Ryan." I decided to recalibrate my mindset and ruminate with confidence on what my knowledgeable trainer told me: "Ryan, resistance is the necessary means to an end. It will all work out in your favor." Physically speaking, it is impossible to grow stronger without feeling the resistance of the weight. In the same way, God allows you and me to follow Him through all the painful life experiences with a purpose in mind. Like a good trainer, He knows the resistance, pressure, and heavy weight of it all is ultimately working in your favor and for your good (see Romans 8:28). Will you listen to the counsel of His grace and trust Jesus?

Why do a large percentage of those who join a gym end up canceling their membership? One word: resistance. It's the same in life. Most who feel resistance lose hope and quit. But it does not have to end this way. We can 100 percent power through life's resistance by praying with and trusting our Friend and Trainer—Jesus.

When you are weak, Jesus can powerfully work within you (see Colossians 1:29). The resistance faced in financial storms is never enjoyable, but if you will trust God to supply all your needs according to His riches (see Philippians 4:19), He will strengthen your resolve. The resistance endured with health challenges is always tiring, but prayerfully believing "I am healed" (see 1 Peter 2:24) will help unleash hope, increase faith, and establish your well-being. Job uncertainties, daily stresses, and unresolved relationship conflicts can all be super wearisome, but hoping in God, that He will keep you in perfect peace (see Isaiah 26:3), settles your mind and emotions under the pressure of resistance.

Perhaps the point of God testing you is because He loves you enough to help you grow in your God-given potential. The pain of resistance is never easy but always essential for growth. *When you are weak*, turn your painful experiences and worries into prayerful deliberations.

Turn Your Worry into Prayer

Dear Jesus, thank You that when I feel weak, Your strength is made known to me. I am sorry for relying on my limited energy. Please help me to wholeheartedly trust Your training while struggling under the weight of resistance. I am turning to You now and turning my worry into prayer. I am fully confident in You. In Jesus' name, amen.

Greater Things

"You will see greater things."
—Jesus, John 1:50 NIV

Winter. Spring. Summer. Autumn. Do you have a favorite season? I live in the Pacific Northwest and absolutely love the beauty of our summertime season. Though summer is my favorite, I have learned to appreciate the greatness of all the seasons.

One summer weekend, since I live near Mount Rainier National Park, I took my family on an adventure hike to the fabulous Grove of the Patriarchs. Seeing trees rising hundreds of feet in the sky that were over one thousand years old reminded me of the profundity and particulars of germination. The Douglas firs were all evidence of being rooted, cultivated, and empowered as the forest's fortified patriarchs. While eating lunch and taking family pictures surrounded by the sheer beauty of the awe-inspiring forestry, I imagined what the towering trees would look like if seen through the perspective of an iPhone time-lapse video, from seedling to soaring. In creative contemplation, the thought occurred to me: like a germinating seed that is buried and broken, there are necessary seasons in life that will feel dark and lonely.

During difficult times when your situation or circumstance is seemingly unfavorable, it will appear as if everyone around you is walking all over you. It is in these uncomfortable places of feeling buried and broken with discouragement that we must remember the words of Jesus planted deep within the soil of the heart: "You will see *greater things.*" It may feel like you will be buried forever, but you are *actually* planted for greatness. It may appear as if your seed dream is broken, but it is *actually* germinating greatly. Dear reader, keep calm and remember that the process of breaking always precedes the promise of blessing. God is undoubtedly in the process of raising you up to a higher level of living—*greater things.*

> *Like a seed that sprouts up out of the depths, when you press through your darkest season and come up as an overcomer, your life will be a beautiful blossom and expression of God's glory within you.*

As you break through—and come out of—the anxiety, fear, and worry, you will gloriously see that all the crud, manure, and mess you dealt with was favorably part of experiencing *greater things*—your personal growth, ordained purpose, and God-given promise for abundant life. Anxiety, fear, and worry do not have to hold you back and hamper your potential any longer. Wherever you feel the weakest, be encouraged that it is in this place where God can prove His sovereignty and strength the most. Prayerfully believe and declare Jesus' hopeful words: "You will see *greater things.*"

Turn Your Worry into Prayer

Dear Jesus, thank You for Your Word planted deep in my heart. I am sorry for not trusting You. I confess my doubts, anxieties, fears, and worries. Please help me with my unbelief. I am turning to You now and turning my worry into prayer. Despite my bad breaks, I prayerfully believe for *greater things* in the days ahead. Thank You, in advance, for *greater things.* Please grow me up in You. In Jesus' name, amen.

Together

*And let us not neglect our meeting together, as some
people do, but encourage one another.*

—*Hebrews 10:25* NLT

Have you ever broken a bone? My middle son, Gavin, has broken more bones than all of my other kids combined.

Not too long ago, Gavin broke his pinky while playing Gaga Ball at recess (Google "Gaga Ball" if you don't know what this game is). Despite his broken finger, with a signature Gavin tenacity, he remained all in, powered through, and wholeheartedly kept playing until he won the match. After receiving an urgent call from his school nurse, I learned of the severity, picked him up, and sped him to the emergency room where the orthopedic doctor took a series of X-rays. Gavin's doctor decided to put him in a six-week *buddy wrap* instead of a traditional cast. Gavin was super glad about this decision, since it was almost summertime and he was looking forward to swimming. A *buddy wrap* meant securely wrapping the broken finger *together* with a strong finger right next to it—with the purpose of creating stability, healing, and ultimately wholeness and strength.

Get this: the orthopedic doctor's name was Dr. Pastor. Coincidence? I think not. Adamant about the pinky finger healing, Dr. Pastor advised, "All deforming happens outward; the closer the fingers the better." In the same way, we are a broken people and desperately in need of internal healing. Moreover, Dr. Pastor's advice encourages us all that we are strongest only when we stick close *together*.

Through the worldwide COVID-19 pandemic, which included economic uncertainty and proliferated racial tension and turmoil, people had an opportunity to either grow further apart and weaker or grow closer in community and stronger. Which has proven true for you? Do you have a growing community of faith where you can buddy wrap or be buddy wrapped *together* with someone else?

Because brokenness leads to deforming when unattended, God never wants any of us to be left isolated and alone. The closer we can be in a healthy community, the better we will become because together equals renewed strength. We is always greater than me.

In the same way Dr. Pastor buddy wrapped my son's broken finger, Jesus buddy wraps us in our brokenness and heals our deepest wounds when we remain *together* in community with both God and people. I've learned some of the greatest brokenness and disjointedness happens when others hurt you and leave you feeling all alone—but it doesn't have to end that way. Healing and health happen when we forgive the offenses of others and remain close-knit with a unifying spirit of *togetherness*. Like Dr. Pastor, the Jewish writer of Hebrews exhorted you and me to stay *together*, connected with the sole life purpose of encouraging joy, peace, happiness, and well-being. This is 100 percent possible when we encourage one another *together*.

Dear reader, there are times when I have been downright upset, angry, and resentful toward others. Times when I've been worried sick and indignant about what has happened to me. But in honest prayer, Dr. Jesus took an X-ray of my deepest hurt and personally came alongside me and buddy wrapped my brokenness back to health.

Perhaps a bad break in life has caused you a great deal of hurt and pain. Maybe you have found yourself broken and in need of some buddy wrapping. Relationship heartache, sickness and disease, financial hardship, and job stresses can easily lead to deep wounds and cause a great amount of anxious brokenness. Scripture reminds us that self-centered arguments and disputes will only leave us in broken divisiveness, but there is great hope, help, healing, and strength in *togetherness*. If you need Jesus to buddy wrap you, it's as easy as saying a prayer: "Jesus, please help." Furthermore, connecting with a Jesus-centered, Bible-based church community will help your mental health and well-being as well as allow you to be like Jesus and buddy wrap others in need.

Dear reader, be encouraged; turning your worry into prayer with other Jesus followers will turn your *me* thinking upside down, and you will suddenly realize the restorative power of *we*. It truly is amazing the reformation that occurs when we come *together*—we > me.

Turn Your Worry into Prayer

Dear Jesus, I am turning to You now and turning my worry into prayer. Thank You for buddy wrapping me with Your forgiveness and loving-kindness. Thank You for being patient with me and continually restoring me. I know disjointed deforming happens when I'm isolated and alone; please help me to remain *together* in relationship with You and others. Help me to love God and people just like You do. In Jesus' name, amen.

God Will Help You

*"Don't get worked up about what may or may
not happen tomorrow. God will help you deal with whatever
hard things come up when the time comes."*
—Jesus, Matthew 6:34

Have you ever spent much time worrying about things that
never ended up happening? I confess that I have.

At times, we allow what may or may not happen to cause us
to get all worked up with a sense of worry, fear, anxiety, and stress.
For example, imagining the outcome to be nothing but negative
when dealing with relationship challenges can cause a great deal of
uneasiness inside you. Overanalyzing financial setbacks and work
pressures can easily trigger a series of fears. Ruminating on your
health problems or a chronic debilitating disease can be stressors
that deeply impact your emotional well-being. Medical studies
have shown that worrying uses up a substantial amount of the
body's energy and depletes the mind of health. Knowing this, Jesus
encouraged us not to get all worked up about the challenges we face.

Dear reader, here is some pragmatic advice: before you dive
into the happenings, pushbacks, and challenges today will bring,
consider Jesus' practical techniques for successful living. Whatever
you are facing, be encouraged; if you pray and turn your worry back
over to Him, *God will help you* deal with it. The heart of this truth
is rooted in intimate relationship. Jesus longs for us to *steep* our life
in His abundance, His healing, and His provision.

Every night in beautiful Seattle, I like to unwind from the
day's endeavors by enjoying a few minutes of meditation and prayer

with a hot cup of my favorite green tea. The longer I allow the bag of tea to steep in the boiling hot water, the more my tea saturates and infuses my meditative prayer experience with an abundance of aromatic flavor. In the same way, I have learned that the more time you spend in personal relationship with Jesus, *steeping* in Him, the more His all-consuming love will transform and fulfill your prayer life. But what does *steeping* in Jesus look like, from a practical everyday standpoint?

Steeping in Jesus is when we take a few minutes each day to pray (talk with God), read the Bible (meditate on God's Word), and worship (express gratitude and thanks to God). My experience has proven the quality of life only gets better as you soak and saturate yourself in relationship with Jesus. If you are broke, busted, or disgusted; stressed, depressed, or confused, there is no better time than the present for immersing yourself in the hope of Jesus. Praying your situation back to God—*steeping* in Jesus—is the prime place where *God will help you*. Fill your mind with this hopeful encouragement the next time you brew a cup of tea:

> *Taking a few extra minutes to steep your mind in prayer will make today taste that much better. God will help you settle whatever bitter things are upsetting you and fill your heart with the comfort of His peace.*

If you are anxious, maybe a good *steeping* in Jesus will refill your mind with the promise of His peace. If you are worried, perhaps a good soaking in the Scripture will help saturate your soul with the joy of Jesus. Your happiness and well-being are ultimately assured by experiencing His presence. Take it to heart, dear reader, and be encouraged, the warmth of God's never-ending love will 100 percent change your life for the better. If you will take a few extra minutes to pray, *God will help you*. He loves you that much.

Turn Your Worry into Prayer

Dear Jesus, please help. I'm sorry for worrying again. I am turning to You now and turning my worry into prayer. By *steeping* in You, I know *God will help me*. I trust that by prayerfully being saturated in relationship with You, the quality of my life will be all the better. I believe that by *steeping* in You there will, in time, be turnaround in my health, relationships, and finances. In turn, please use the evidence in my changed life to help other people find and follow You too. In Jesus' name, amen.

Before the Master

Get down on your knees before the Master;
it's the only way you'll get on your feet.
—James 4:10

Have you ever physically knelt down in prayer? If so, when was the last time? One version of today's familiar text articulated by James, the brother of Jesus, says when you humble yourself before the Lord, He will lift you up. In a nutshell, kneeling is a sure way to consciously humble yourself and be blessed by God in return.

The Old Testament prophet Daniel lived out this timeless truth; he would routinely kneel down in prayer three times a day, giving thanks to God (see Daniel 6:10). The relatable part of Daniel's story is that he lived in a culture of opinionated people who actively opposed him. Daniel lived in a nation full of politics, proliferated racial tension, and segregating turmoil. Furthermore, he lived during a time of unrest with an ever-increasing amount of citywide hopelessness. Sound familiar? Daniel's respose was 100 percent courageous and countercultural. Despite the resistance he faced from a self-saturated people who threatened not just his freedom but even his life if he continued living for God, Daniel repeatedly got down on his knees *before the Master* and prayed with a thankful heart. In other words, despite his conflicting fears, he turned his worry into prayer and faithfully kept God first in his life.

Fact: Prayer works and is the only way you can get on up, on your good foot. In my experience, kneeling *before the Master* is an outward expression of an inward confidence that notably displaces worry and displays a wholehearted trust in God.

Some time ago, I decided to try praying the Daniel 6:10 way—three times a day. I strategically set three alarms on my Apple Watch: 6:10 a.m., 12:10 p.m., and 6:10 p.m. (Thank God for a watch that reminds me to pray when I'm way too busy.) Three times a day, wherever I'm at, I purposefully get down on my knees *before the Master* and prayerfully take the stance of gratitude and thanksgiving. As I humbly kneel, emptying my mind of everything that I have been struggling with, I give Jesus all my worries with believing prayer. I consciously hope with faith and an unceasing dependence on Him for joy, peace, courage, and strength to stand. This prayer discipline only takes a few minutes throughout the day and has completely changed my life. I have come to learn that kneeling *before the Master* is a sure way to inspire faith and raise your hopes up out of negative, anxious, fearful, and worrisome living.

Be encouraged, dear reader, that when you feel down to nothing, God is still up to something and is working in your favor. Get down on your knees before the Master, and you will see how turning your worry into prayer changes everything in your soul for the better.

Prayer *before the Master* will raise your mind up out of your seemingly impossible situation and steady your feet through the not-so-great circumstances you are facing . . . if you will prayerfully kneel before Jesus aware of your need for Him. Truth be told, a surrendered heart to Jesus is the sure way to a fulfilled and happy life. Dear reader, be encouraged; it starts very simply with a humble prayer like "Jesus, please help." Will you pray now?

Turn Your Worry into Prayer

Dear Jesus, thank You for another day of possibility. I express my utmost trust in You by humbly kneeling in Your presence. Please forgive my inconsistencies and ungratefulness in prayer. I am turning to You now and turning my worry into prayer. I will slow down, get down on my knees *before the Master*, and get up to face the day confident and worry-free. In Jesus' name, amen.

God Is Near Us Whenever We Pray

The LORD our God is near us
whenever we pray to Him.
—Deuteronomy 4:7 *NIV*

Have you ever wrestled with feeling lonely and isolated? Living disconnected and remaining alone can ultimately lead people to being held captive in a place of hopelessness and static distress.

Like a radio out of frequency, there are times in life when we find ourselves anxiously searching for clarity because we have tuned out to prayer and tuned in to worry. From radio waves and microwaves to television, cell phone, and satellites, hundreds of thousands of frequency waves are all around us. For us to see, hear, and experience these frequency waves, we need to be tuned in. Whether by way of cell phone reception, Wi-Fi, or radio, I'm sure, like me, you hate being disconnected and want nothing more than to remain connected and clearly tuned in.

Prayer is the frequency and connection point that tunes us in to fully knowing and experiencing the waves of God's life-giving Spirit. Scripture promises that God is noticeably near us whenever we pray.

Allow this ancient text to encourage health, unleash hope, and inspire faith in you today. This is a powerful truth we can contemplate and a frequency we can all connect to. How is *your* prayer life? Are *you* tuned in to Jesus-centered prayer?

When you prayerfully tune in, dear reader, remember to keep it honest, keep it simple, and keep it going. It really is that easy. Praying allows for breakthrough in the heavenlies that brings change on earth in your life in a very real way. Your faith-filled prayer exchange with Jesus is literally the breeding ground for God to harvest miracles in your everyday life. *God is near us whenever we pray.*

Moreover, prayer that is tuned in is simple and intimate conversation between you and Jesus that aligns the way you do things with the way God does things. Prayer is extraordinary. It allows Jesus to add His "extra" to your "ordinary." Prayer is supernatural. It allows Jesus to add His "super" to your "natural." In the same way my children can easily connect with me by either calling or texting, as a child of Father God, you can easily connect with Him through prayer. Prayer connects us to the frequency of Jesus' loving-kindness, reassuring us again and again that *God is near us whenever we pray.*

Be encouraged, dear reader, if you happen to be facing agonizing sorrow, are troubled with anxiousness, or have experienced a recent setback, you can tune in to an entirely new frequency of hope, joy, and peace by taking a minute to start a dialogue with Jesus. He is much nearer than you may think. If you pray, God will answer.

Turn Your Worry into Prayer

Dear Jesus, thank You that You are near me whenever I pray. I'm sorry for not praying more. I am turning to You now and turning my worry into prayer. Please help me remember to pray a few times throughout the day to ensure I am tuned out to my worry and tuned in to Your peace. I love You with my whole heart and commit to trusting You more in prayer. In Jesus' name, amen.

Be Anxious for Nothing

*Be anxious for nothing, but in everything by prayer
and supplication, with thanksgiving, let your
requests be made known to God.*
—*Philippians 4:6 NKJV*

Did you know there is a pandemic even greater than COVID-19? Millions of people worldwide have found themselves infected with a mind sickness called anxiety. Have you ever experienced its effects? Maybe responsibilities or work apprehensions have you anxiously tied in knots. Intrapersonal and interpersonal conflicts can be the cause of deep turmoil. Perhaps unexpected budgetary challenges and the pressures of having to refigure your finances are at the forefront of reoccurring worry and dreadful defeat.

Are the thoughts you continually ruminate on afflictive and emotionally harmful? Have you been stuck in a cycle of tension and wrestling within? We tend to engage our inner thoughts like they are videos being played on repeat. These fear-driven movies of the mind are produced with an inner agitation that frightfully underscores the scenes of our unsatisfied and unhappy lives. What are you anxious about, and why do you worry so much?

Anxiety is truly a myriad of afflictive thoughts, negative inner feelings, and unpleasant tensions within the mind, body, and spirit that may never really happen. Like a nervous pianist at their debut concert performance, anxiety is fed by the negative inner mind movies and the "I'm going to fail" thoughts that we tend to repeatedly play. Over and over, the psychodrama and negative patterns of the afflicted mind add to the fear and worry like a cancerous mass of anxiety inside.

Our thoughts about the situation prove far worse than the actual situation itself. The antidote: prayer—talk with Jesus about everything in your life. Be confident and consistent with the practice of prayer because God *really* wants to help you succeed. Each of us are built, designed, and created by God to practice prayerful contemplation.

In the same way practicing the piano daily was fundamental for me to learn how to play with inner confidence, practicing prayerful contemplation daily is key for me to live with inner peace.

God invites you, right now, not to worry (contemplate afflictive thoughts) about anything but to pray (contemplate Jesus' thoughts) about everything; tell Jesus what you need, and be sure to thank Him (grateful thoughts) for all He does. Starting within the mind, the Lord changes everything when we pray; quite literally, *every thing* changes. Dear reader, will you *be anxious for nothing* and start to practice turning your worry into prayer? If prayer wonderfully works for me, surely it will wondrously work for you too.

Turn Your Worry into Prayer

Dear Jesus, I am turning to You now and turning my worry into prayer. I'm sorry for entertaining my afflictive thoughts and ask that You please help me to slow down long enough to listen, hear, and rest in Your promised peace. I trust my contemplative prayer and daily meditation practice will change everything in my life for the better. Please help transform my mind by reorienting the thoughts I reflect on. In Jesus' name, amen.

Will You Ask Him?

*"If you, then, though you are evil, know how to give good
gifts to your children, how much more will your Father in
heaven give good gifts to those who ask him!"*
—Jesus, Matthew 7:11 NIV

What is the greatest, most faith-filled request you have ever asked God for? Not too long ago I had taken my family to experience Disneyland. We had a fabulous day enjoying thrilling roller coasters and over-priced fantasy food and, of course, chasing after the mouse that started it all for the perfect family picture. After a rewarding day of adventure and cardio, walking nearly nine miles, my daughter, Lilly, desperately wanted me to carry her out of the park. With those tired yet beautiful brown eyes, she convincingly looked up and confidently asked, "Daddy, could you please carry me?" How could I deny her genuine and heartfelt request? I jokingly asked her right back, "Sweet-P, if I carry you, who will carry me?" Full of wit and without missing a beat, she boldly said, "Jesus will carry you, Daddy."

The next time we find ourselves weary and burdened, instead of picking up the phone to find refuge in more busyness, let's try going to the throne to ask the Father for His help. Let's forego the dialogue with everyone else, where we tend to institutionalize disappointment, and go straight to Father God in hopeful prayer.

Like Lilly, do you understand the *"ask Him"* promise from our heavenly Father in Matthew 7:11? Perhaps a visit to Saint Matthew's 7-Eleven has the Big Gulp blessing your thirsty soul needs. If you are weary, revisit the idea of asking God for a refill of peace in exchange for your suffering, hardship, difficulty, and worry.

Do you need protection? *Ask Him!* Do you need healing from physical or emotional pain? *Ask Him!* Do you need help with your job or provision amidst unemployment? *Ask Him!* Do you need dating advice or marital support? *Ask Him!* Worrying about these things will do nothing but upset you and cause more angst. Anxiously complaining to others will only accentuate your disappointments. By the way, long wordy prayers are not necessary and only prolong answers. Short, pocket-sized prayers work best and foster the Father's blessing and favor. Like Lilly, when you are tired, worn out, burned out, and in need, make every effort to *ask Him* for help. Jesus promised the Father will give good gifts to everyone who will simply *ask Him*. In the same way Lilly asked to be carried, all you need to do is trust Jesus and confidently *ask Him* to carry you. Will you ask Him? No one can give you a pick-me-up like Jesus. Let's give uplifting prayer a try together.

Turn Your Worry into Prayer

Dear Jesus, could You please carry me? Whether it's in my relationships, health, family, or finances, I am truly in need for You to intervene with Your supernatural wisdom and strength. Please forgive me for forgetting to ask You for help along the way. I am turning to You now and turning my worry into prayer. Jesus, I ask because I confidently believe You will answer me with good and gracious gifts from the Father above. May Your joy refill my thirsty soul and Your peace carry me through with happiness and well-being. In Jesus' name, amen.

Trusting in God

The fear of human opinion disables;
trusting in GOD protects you from that.
—Proverbs 29:25

How often do you compare yourself with someone else based on opinion? Just the other day, I was seriously sidetracked by a person's opinion about my driving in a parking lot. Focusing on the judgmental opinion this very angry and animated person was yelling at me, I lost my footing getting out of my car, tripped on the curb, and sprained my ankle. In the same way, it is easy to get sidetracked by all the loud opinions from other. I have learned that relying on the opinions of other people to define how you think can cause you to lose your focus and trip you up.

It's far too easy to lose balance in life and trip on the curb of negative comparisons when repeating the inner mind movies and thinking on others' opinions. Social media, for example, is full of opinions that we repeatedly scroll through. If we aren't careful, we can suddenly find our distracted focus has tripped us up on the curb of insecurity, resulting in another sprain of comparison—comparing the best of their life with the worst of yours. Furthermore, the fear of

> *The ancient remedy and first aid to our disabling insecurities and sprains of comparison is trusting, not in human opinion, but in God.*

failure and the fear of rejection are resultant comparisons. Fear of failure destroys self-image, and the fear of rejection destroys self-esteem. Ouch!

Dear reader, the centermost chapter in the Bible highlights the main substance of our healing: "It is better to *trust* in the LORD than to put confidence in man" (Psalm 118:8 KJV, emphasis added). Securing your value on human opinion will honestly just trip you up with anxiety. Anxiety can be defined as divided thinking, mixed emotion, and paralyzed will—debilitating your thought life at best.

People's opinions are ever changing, just like the people who voice them. What if, with Jesus' help, you emptied your mind of all those negative opinions, comparisons, and fear thoughts by prayerfully *trusting in God*? Be encouraged, "their" (insert the name of the person who has you second-guessing how you do things) opinion of you is not the final word.

Here is the lesson that has changed my life: the less you care about *their* opinion, the happier and healthier you will be. Giving all your cares to God in prayer will give you a new sense of security and strength. *Trusting in God* through prayer stabilizes you from being tripped up with insecurity, sprained with comparison, and disabled by all the negative opinions of others. Prayer reorients you to live genuinely happy and free of all anxiety, fear, and worry. Be encouraged, dear reader, *trusting in God* is the secret that will transform your mind and empower you to walk carefree in His care.

Turn Your Worry into Prayer

Dear Jesus, please help me to empty all my negative fear thoughts and align my mind with the positive faith thoughts that are found in Your holy Word. I am turning to You now and turning my worry into prayer. I'm sorry for getting tripped up and not wholeheartedly trusting in You. Forgive me for comparing myself with others. I know Your opinion of me is most important. By *trusting in God*, I am living confident in Your everlasting love and care. In Jesus' name, amen.

Ask God for It

*You don't have what you want
because you don't ask God for it.*
—*James 4:2* NLT

On a scale of 1 to 10, how happy and fulfilled are you? Most people want nothing more than to be happy and satisfied in life. If you are agitated or unhappy about anything in your life, there is an ancient remedy guaranteed to help you.

Not too long ago I was working out during a family vacation at our resort gym. The temperature was borderline unbearable due to the thermostat being broken. I overheard the overheated guests complaining about how hot it was. Despite everyone being agitated and unhappy, I was surprised that not one person had taken the initiative to address the issue at hand and ask the hotel management for help. In an obviously tense and grossly sweaty situation, I decided to take our problem to the front desk personnel who, in turn, responded by saying, "Happy to help—we're on it!"

In the same way, God is willing, available, and happy to help if we will simply ask Him. Instead of talking to everyone else about the problem, try praying to God about it. The Scriptures deduce that you will 100 percent fix the temperature of your unsatisfied life and have exactly what you need if you will simply *ask God for it.* An agitated heart that is devoid of joy, peace, happiness, and well-being will spend a lifetime searching for it—I know so because I have tried so.

When we seek happiness in education, position, popularity, social acceptance, money, sex, substance abuse, food medicating, and exercise, we're left undone. The resultant aftermath proves these unsatisfying methods leave us still in need of a solution.

If the prayer thermostat in your life is broken, the heat of anxiety and worry will continue rising to an unbearable temperature, leaving the soul in despair. But it doesn't have to end this way. Help is available.

Like the gym guests whose sweaty complaints just multiplied, when unremedied, our unhappiness overflows and splashes onto others around us, only making matters worse.

In the same way the front desk employee willingly said, "Happy to help—we're on it!" God is on it and ready to help. If you are suffering and need healing, stop sweating it and *ask God for it*. If you need financial provision, stop the burn of worry and *ask God for it*. If you need peace amid a relationship conflict, *ask God for it*. Dear reader, if you don't have what you want in life, simply *ask God for it* in prayer. He is happy to help.

Turn Your Worry into Prayer

Dear Jesus, thank You for Your help. I am sorry for complaining and grumbling and looking to the temporal for my satisfaction. I am turning to You now and turning my worry into prayer. Today I remember how important it is to personally connect with You in prayer. I understand that when I have not, it's because I ask not, so I boldly ask You now for help in my health, finances, and relationship matters. Please help, Lord. In Jesus' name, amen.

It's All Good

*And we know that in all things God works for
the good of those who love him, who have
been called according to his purpose.*
—*Romans 8:28 NIV*

Have you ever found yourself irritated and upset that other people seemingly don't have to deal with all the same problems and setbacks you do? "Why am *I* left with all the bad breaks, and *they* seem to get all the good ones?" It's not a wishing of ill will or malice toward others, but a sincere desire and honest longing to be valued and promoted. You are not alone; God is still with you, working all things favorably for your highest good.

As a musician, music theory has taught me the minor second interval. A minor second interval is that dissonant sound you hear when two different notes right next to each other are played together. When scored with dark emotion and staccato dynamics, it is meant to sound inharmonious and feel jarring. If you have ever watched the movie *Jaws*, you can recall John Williams' popular theme song as one of the most memorable minor second compositions: *Duunnn-dunnn. Duuuuunnn-duun. Dun-dun, dun-dun, dun-dun, dun-dun!* This minor second experience invokes sharp scary teeth, fear, worry, and death. *Jaws* undoubtedly leaves you feeling as if it's *not* all good.

However, the same minor second interval can be played with an entirely different purpose that articulates a sound of hope. In 1810, Ludwig van Beethoven wrote "Für Elise" (For Elise), one of his most popular compositions, for Elizabeth whom he loved and wanted to marry. *Dun-dun, dun-dun, dun-dun, dun-dun, dun.* Beethoven's minor second score and heartfelt expression enunciate joy and romance, life and love. "Für Elise" leaves you feeling like everything is going to be all right and that *it's all good.* The difference between the two minor second song experiences is simply the author's intended purpose of the score.

In the same way, instead of hearing your challenges as the death of you, know that Jesus is the author and finisher of our faith and is working behind the scenes at writing your life's score. He is composing with a tone of hope because He is working every dissonant note in your favor. Despite the anxious feelings of your current tension, have faith that *it's all good*! Just like you and me, many people throughout the ancient biblical narrative were seemingly swallowed up by setbacks and felt defeated by their deathly despondency. But God . . .

> *The enemy wants nothing more than for despairing minor second dissonance, accented with depressive dynamics, to be the mark of the score of your life. But what the enemy works for your harm, God reworks for your good. Dear reader, it's all good.*

God is not finished reorienting your minor second composition. If it's not all good, it's not all done. He's still working it all out for your highest good. Your minor second situation is beautiful when entrusted to the hands of the Master, Jesus.

Be encouraged, dear reader, to turn your worry into prayer and remain thankful. Jesus wants nothing more than for you to know covenant relationship with Him and to experience His loving-kindness. *It's all good.*

Turn Your Worry into Prayer

Dear Jesus, I am turning to You now and turning my worry into prayer. I'm sorry for, at times, relying on my own understanding and not wholeheartedly believing Your promise that *it's all good*. I am trusting You that my minor second situation is being scored with my highest good in mind, and that Your love will ultimately lead me toward a turnaround victory. In Jesus' name, amen.

God's Got This

"I know what I'm doing. I have it all planned
out—plans to take care of you, not abandon you,
plans to give you the future you hope for."
—God, Jeremiah 29:11

Have you ever been really disappointed about a setback in life that happened? Maybe you prayed for a friend or loved one who ended up not getting well. Perhaps you worked extra hard for a job promotion that ended up falling through. Or possibly you believed for a relationship to work out and it never did. We all experience deep disappointment when things seemingly do not work out. Despite the setbacks faced, you can confidently know God still has a really good plan with your best interest in mind.

Not too long ago, I remember watching my father labor through stage 4 colon cancer, which led to physical hardship and suffering chemotherapy treatments. Following a short cancer remission and celebrated victory, I distinctly remember my dad standing in front of the family with the upsetting news of yet another tumor being found. Can you relate to me when I asked Jesus, "Really, God? This? *Again?*" Despite his required brain surgery, my dad and mom courageously led the way in declaring, "*God's got this!*" Dad's fortified faith in God's plan, as mysterious as it is, had deafened his ear to all the disparaging remarks of the adversary and the skeptical defeatists. Where does your faith lie when looking in the eyes of your greatest fear?

In the same way my dad faced the unknown and seemingly

impossible by intentionally ignoring all the negativity, be encouraged to keep your spirit tuned in to God's promise. If there is one thing I've learned while walking with my family through these difficult situations and disappointing circumstances, I can trust *God's got this*. What pain has affected you and is causing a great deal of fear and anxiety? Dear reader, like my dad declared, say it three times and believe it: "*God's got this!*"

In the same way my dad had a painful brain tumor that required surgical removal to keep him alive, worry is a cancer that causes pain in your head and desperately needs to be prayerfully removed to keep your hope alive.

Moreover, like a surgery patient would never surrender their body to an ignorant doctor, you can courageously stand confident with Dr. Jesus, believing He is more than able with a sure plan that will undoubtedly help you in the right way at the right time. Whatever physical, relational, emotional, or spiritual cares you are presently living with, trust Jesus with your life by turning your worry into prayer. This is the sure way forward toward the future you hope for. The secret to maintaining your sunny and joyful disposition despite life's vicissitudes is prayer—*God's got this!*

Turn Your Worry into Prayer

Dear Jesus, thank You for the surety of a good plan in You. I'm sorry for losing faith and giving up hope at times. I am turning to You now and turning my worry into prayer. Please help me to be energized with Your spirit of positivity. I give You my anger, fear, and pain. It is my desire for You, Dr. Jesus, to help me overcome my cancerous anxiety, fear, and worry. I want to see Your perfect plan come true in my life. I want to overflow abundant hope with others. I want to believe *God's got this*. So, please, help my unbelief. In Jesus' name, amen.

Come and Talk with Me

My heart has heard you say, "Come and talk with me."
And my heart responds, "LORD, I am coming."
—Psalm 27:8 NLT

Have you ever ignored a phone call from a loved one because of being way too busy? If you are anything like me, I am a busy person with a very busy schedule. For this reason, I love waking up early and taking time to meditate. Along with my morning workout at the gym, I enjoy contemplative prayer. Because of the daily onslaught of demands and challenges encountered, one of my favorite nonnegotiable things to do is talk with Jesus over coffee.

Prayer has not come naturally to me. With a willingness to get up early, a tenacity to try again after failing, and a discipline to just keep showing up, resultant is observable evidence and proof of all the benefits of prayer in my life. Responding to the invitation and call of God has repeatedly taught me that time spent talking with Jesus is time well invested.

With honesty and brokenness I often pray, "Lord, I am coming . . ." All of my hurts, habits, and hang-ups, all of my sin, I bring it all to Jesus because He wants to save me from it all. Answering the invitation of Jesus is my heartfelt response to an inner prodding and calling: *"Come and talk with Me."* Simply put, *coffee with Jesus* is my response to His personal bidding. Did you know He's calling you too? Dear reader, Jesus loves you.

We all experience seasons of hardship and pain. I can remember days gone by when each of my children had been stifled with stressors. Especially in the formative years of learning, growing, and gleaning, challenges can often seem too much to bear. The tear-stained eyes. The colossal frustration. The resultant disappointment. I've learned, regardless of age, we all can relate to pain. Being an encourager, my instant response to my kiddos (especially my daughter, Lilly) during their setbacks was, and continues to be, to extend an invitation to come alongside and ensure them I am here to help. As a hugger, in my loving invitation and echoing of *"Come and talk with me,"* I also include, "Let's hug it out!" In the same way, our heavenly Father is calling out and wanting to surround you with care through prayer.

Are there health struggles, financial challenges, relationship issues, job frustrations, or other setbacks that have proven overwhelming in your life? Whether a sprained finger, bruised spirit, or shattered dream, each of us will at some point face hardship and pain, difficulty and distress that require remedy. Be encouraged, it doesn't have to end in frustration and disappointment. In the same way I extend the invitation to my kids to come, talk, and "hug it out," God wants nothing more than for you to respond to His healing touch—*"Come and talk with Me."*

As a child of the Most High God, take time to answer your Father's call and talk with Him. Turn your worry into prayer and find hope in the Lord Jesus Christ. Whether responding in a time of stress or offense, frustration or disappointment, may your heart be encouraged by prayerfully answering His loving call of *"Come and talk with Me"* with a hopeful *"Lord, I am coming."*

Turn Your Worry into Prayer

Dear Jesus, I am thankful for Your loving invitation to talk together. I am sorry for not responding to Your call sooner. I am turning to You now and turning my worry into prayer. With all my cares and concerns—big and small—I come. With all my broken and afflictive thoughts, I come. With all my negative inner feelings and unpleasant tension felt within my body and mind, I come. Please help me. In Jesus' name, amen.

Keep On Waiting—It Will Happen!

"At the time I have decided, my words will come true.
You can trust what I say about the future. It may take a
long time, but keep on waiting—it will happen!"
—God, Habakkuk 2:3 CEV

What prayers have you been waiting a long time for God to answer? Whether your driven prayers have led you to a green-light yes, a red-light no, or a yellow-light not yet answer, I echo the ancient Jewish writer Habakkuk's foresight and prolific Good News to *keep on waiting—it will happen!* In God's perfect timing, in this life or the next, He promises your breakthrough will come. Get your hopes up and get ready for what Jesus is about to do next in your life.

Identical to Habakkuk, a man who knew what it felt like to wait at a red-light *no*, maybe you have been waiting for a green-light *yes* a long while, calling out to God, "How long, O Lord, must I call for Your help?" Be encouraged, He hears all your prayers and sees your frustrations due to fruitlessness. Stand your ground with a faith-filled heart, watching and waiting for His promised answers. If unemployed (trust me, I have also experienced the yellow-light *not yet* uncertainty of waiting), *keep on waiting—it will happen!* As your patience begins to wear thin, remember He is omniscient and will favorably work on your behalf because He knows what is best for you. Dear reader, be encouraged, Jesus has a *really* good plan, so you are waiting for a *really* good reason.

Not knowing the real issue at hand, I remember wholeheartedly praying and vehemently asking God to heal my dad of his equilibrium problems. After a series of tests, the doctors discovered that my dad's challenged equilibrium was a direct result from an even greater concern and deeper issue at hand. The real problem was a tumor in his head that required immediate brain surgery. Had God answered my immediate prayer that didn't address the root of the worry, my dad's life would have been threatened by much more than vertigo issues (and a suffering golf handicap). In the same way, could it be that seemingly unanswered prayer is God saying "Not yet" instead of "No"? Just because you haven't seen anything happen yet doesn't mean that you won't.

If the things you have been praying about have not changed, perhaps Jesus is using the things you have been praying about to change you.

In the same way the COVID-19 pandemic taught everyone in the world to patiently endure, remember, dear reader, it's not forever; it's just for now. If you are struggling with disease, *keep on waiting—it will happen!* Say it before you see it, believe it before you receive it, and whatever you do, do not give up hope. As you travail the test of time, keep interceding and earnestly seeking His joy, peace, and loving presence in your life by turning your worry into prayer. In the same way God did with me, the Lord's right answer is coming in the right way and at the right time. There is a perfect plan and place, decided upon by God Almighty, where your miracle moment and answered prayer awaits you. While we don't always get the answer we want, be encouraged to keep the faith. You can trust the Lord with your future. It may take a long time, so *keep on waiting—it will happen!*

Turn Your Worry into Prayer

Dear Jesus, I trust You are working in my favor. I am turning to You now and turning my worry into prayer.

I'm sorry for doubting You and voicing my negative thoughts and opinions. I will patiently wait, knowing my right miracle will happen in the right way at the right time. I say it before I see it and believe it before I receive it. My turnaround breakthrough is coming! In Jesus' name, amen.

He'll Help You Out

*Pile your troubles on God's shoulders—he'll
carry your load, he'll help you out.*
—Psalm 55:22

Who do you turn to when in crisis? Who do you take your troubles to?

Not too long ago I was sipping coffee at a local Seattle restaurant. As I was saying a short prayer with bowed head before enjoying my corned beef hash, I happened to hear my server walk up and place the condiments I had requested on the tabletop. Aware of his arrival, I smiled with eyes wide open and completed the prayer out loud saying, "And thank You, God, for a super awesome server. I ask You to please bless him by helping him today. In Jesus' name, amen."

His response shocked me a bit as he became emotional. "I saw you praying over your meal and hoped you might pray for me as well." Another opportunity to pray—awesome! Whether a God coincidence or confirmation, how cool is that?

After I inquired, he told me of many troubles he was personally carrying and professionally worrying about. I went on to encourage him with *"He'll help you out."* This was the encouraging scriptural truth I had *coincidentally* read a few minutes earlier in my midmorning Bible meditation.

I have come to learn that Jesus willingly answers the needs of everyone who will pile all their anxieties, fears, and worries on His shoulders in prayer.

On the same day as this revealingly powerful prayer occurrence, my dad underwent brain surgery for the removal of a cancerous tumor. I encouraged him with the same hopeful promise I had shared earlier at the restaurant. "Dad, *He'll help you out.*" Whether it's a server's cares and concerns or a severe cancer diagnosis, all of us at some point will need help carrying our pile of troubles. Be encouraged, dear reader, the Lord Jesus Christ will carry your load—*He'll help you out.*

Less than forty-eight hours after my dad's surgery, he was released from the hospital and, with much care and prayer, steadily improved. In the same way, dear reader, with God you are going to get through whatever you are facing.

I'm writing this as knowledge-based, research-based observable evidence and fact: when you are struggling to carry your tray of troubles any further, and when you are too weary to carry on from your bed of burdens, He'll help you out.

If there is one thing I know, no matter how many worries are overwhelming you and weighing you down, God's shoulders are 100 percent broad enough to take on the weight of them all. If you consciously admit that you desperately need His help, *He'll help you out.*

Is there anyone else in the entire world besides Jesus who loves you enough to offer His help with carrying all your problems, including stress and offense, anxiety, fear, and worry? Even if someone were willing, who but Jesus is *actually* able to save, forgive, and heal you? Jesus promises to carry the weight of your burden *if* you will give it to Him in prayer.

The Bible historically gives us thousands and thousands of years of scientific evidence, and I have observed time and time again the proof of this truth. Be encouraged, with absolute and unceasing dependence on God, you can 100 percent count on the fact that *He'll help you out.*

Turn Your Worry into Prayer

Dear Jesus, I appreciate the fact that You are willing to take all my anxiety, fear, and worry. I'm sorry for holding my inner heaviness longer than I should. I am turning to You now and turning my worry into prayer. I pile every afflictive thought, negative inner feeling, and unpleasant emotion, as well as the turmoil within my body and mind, onto Your shoulders. Please help me to trust Your strength instead of my own to carry me through my mess. In Jesus' name, amen.

Take a Real Rest

"Are you tired? Worn out? Burned out on religion?
Come to me. Get away with me and you'll recover your life.
I'll show you how to take a real rest."
—*Jesus, Matthew 11:28*

Have you ever felt heavy-laden and burdened from all of life's cares? When you feel worn out and tired from carrying your insurmountable concerns, worries, and everyday responsibilities, burnout is inevitable. Like the workaholic, are you someone who takes refuge in busyness with a keep on keeping on mindset, despite a fatigued mind, body, and soul that is counseling you with fervency, "Drop it and rest"?

On the last day of class before graduation, the graduate school professor held a glass of water over his head and asked his students, "How heavy is this glass full of water?" After fielding an array of theories, the professor deduced, "The absolute weight of this glass is irrelevant. What supremely matters is how long I hold it. Holding it for a minute or two is one thing, but holding it for an hour is quite another. Eventually, if I continue holding onto it, I will need to *drop it* because the longer I hold it, the heavier it feels to me."

The students all nodded in agreement.

"In the same way," the professor continued, "your mind full of worry, frustration, disappointment, stress, and offense is very much like this glass full of water. Thinking about it for a minute or two is one thing, but thinking about it for an hour or a day is quite another. The only way to find joy, peace, happiness, and well-being again is to *drop it* and *take a real rest.*"

Dear reader, whether it has been a minute, an hour, a day, or a decade, if you have been holding a mind full of cares and concerns, be encouraged to drop it. Jesus is inviting you, "Come . . . *take a real rest.*"

In the same way you can only hold a glass full of water above your head for so long before it feels extremely heavy, I have learned that the longer you hold a mindset full of worry, frustration, disappointment, stress, and offense, the heavier and more unbearable life feels. Dear reader, drop it in prayer and *take a real rest* with Jesus.

As I continue to wrestle daily with carrying a chronic disease like type 1 diabetes, I have discovered the secret to experiencing true peace is to take a real rest with Jesus by dropping my worry in prayer.

Take a Real Rest 101: Stop, drop and pray. STOP all work, DROP your worry, and PRAY. Prayerfully release all tension and worry within you, relinquish your cares and concerns, and get away with Jesus by doing something emotionally enjoyable—pray. Doing so will give your soul a sense of healing, fulfillment, and confidence.

Turn Your Worry into Prayer

Dear Jesus, I am turning to You now and turning my worry into prayer. I'm sorry for not listening and responding sooner. With Your help, I will worship more and worry less, trust Scripture more and stress less, pray more and panic less. I consciously come to You and acknowledge I need to *take a real rest.* Please help me to stop all work, drop my worry, and pray. Help me to relinquish my burdens, cares, and concerns. Like a healing medication, may my every prayerful meditation transform me by renewing my mind to believe that I am healed. In Jesus' name, amen.

The Last Word

When all is said and done, the last word
is Immanuel—God-With-Us.
—Isaiah 8:10

Have you ever experienced a really bad break? I have. Perhaps, like me, you were laid off at the worst possible time. (Is there ever a good time to be laid off?) Maybe your health is not working in your favor and the doctors have diagnosed you with a life-threatening disease. Even worse, like some of my family members and close friends have experienced, maybe the doctor doesn't know how to diagnose you. Moreover, when there have been a series of financial and physical challenges accompanied by arguments, disputes, and relational issues with a spouse or significant other, the compilation of life's vicissitudes can overwhelmingly cause a great deal of anxiety and stress. But I have learned, it does not have to end this way.

When faced with insurmountable impossibilities, rest assured that you are not alone. Despite the people or things that actively oppose you, the force *for* you is much greater than the force *against* you. I've learned that the people who hurt you, though they may even be an authority figure with position and power, have misappropriated influence that simply does not have the last word. I have also learned, as a type 1 diabetic, that the Great Physician, Jesus, is with us to remind us, every day, the chronic sicknesses we contend with and diseases we struggle through do not have the final word. The painful turmoil that, at times, leaves Jesus followers feeling alone is not the period at the end of the sentence. Be encouraged, dear reader, with Jesus on your side, you are never left alone. He promised, "Surely I am with you always, to the very end of the age" (Matthew 28:20 NIV). His Word reigns.

Take a minute or two to quiet your anxious spirit by mediating on this truth. Listen for the Holy Spirit to confirm this within your consciousness. His Word is *the last word.* If God is with you, strength is yours. If God be for you, who can be against you (see Romans 8:31)? Be encouraged, dear reader, any negative word that has ever been spoken over you is broken right now. You are who Jesus says you are, and Jesus says, "You are loved." Always remember, the Most High God is 100 percent with you. You are empowered and have what it takes to carry on. Things can be said and done against you, but the Almighty has *the last word,* and that word is Immanuel—God-with-us.

> *With historical factual evidence and ancient scriptural truth, the biblical narrative proves that the last word in the cosmos will forever be Immanuel—God-with-us.*

Turn Your Worry into Prayer

Dear Jesus, thank You for Your promise to always be with me. It gives me great confidence and assurance through the difficulties to sense You are here with me. Sickness doesn't have the last word. Those who actively oppose me do not have the last word. Even my situation and circumstances do not have the last word. Jesus, You have *the last word,* and that word promises that You are forever with me. I am turning to You now and turning my worry into prayer. In Jesus' name, amen.

Conclusion

I have lived with type 1 diabetes for decades and am still not used to it.

I was relentlessly reminded the other night, after having a dangerously high blood glucose episode that forced me to return home and forfeit a ministry event that I had traveled a far distance from Seattle to attend, type 1 diabetes has a disagreeable mind of its own and is a disease that does not want to be controlled. I am not prepared for *another* long and difficult recovery . . . *again*. Most will never understand this thorn-in-my-side reality that I daily endure (with a joyful Jesus smile, of course).

After being hospitalized several times over the years, rushed to the emergency room on multiple accounts (once in an ambulance after my wife had to desperately call 911 for help), I have learned that living with type 1 diabetes means living with a life-threatening and chronic disease that relentlessly demands attention. Unfortunately, even when I take it seriously and try to manage this unruly disease by doing the right thing, the wrong thing still happens with my blood glucose's unbalanced rebelliousness.

This disorienting and despairing disease has once again forced me to trust God totally. I can 100 percent agree with Paul the Apostle when he confessed, "It was so bad we didn't think we were going to make it. We felt like we'd been sent to death row, that it was all over for us. As it turned out, it was the best thing that could have happened . . . we were forced to trust God totally" (2 Corinthians 1:8-9).

Therefore, once again, I turn my worry into prayer and desperately ask, "Jesus, please help." As a matter of fact, He did. When I returned home around midnight after traveling the long distance back, I found that my family were all upstairs in their beds. Unfortunately, that was not all I found. Had I not had the diabetic episode and returned home from the ministry event, I would not have found that the gas stove had accidentally been left on, apparently for hours, and was dangerously filling the entire house with toxic fumes and deadly gases. As it turns out, turning worry into prayer really works because Jesus lovingly used my diabetic episode to save my family from catastrophic doom.

If there is anything I have learned, it's that everyone is wrestling with some type of hardship. This is part of life on earth. But our place of pain can also be our place of providential prayer. Turning worry into prayer is the secret to finding joy, peace, happiness, and well-being. My personal turnaround experience is observable evidence of this scientific truth. In the same way turning worry into prayer has 100 percent changed my life, Jesus' prayer prescription will transform your life too.

About the Author

Born into a lineage of ministers, Rev. Ryan Bunbury gave his heart to Jesus, was baptized (full immersion) in water, and filled with the Holy Spirit in his formative years. He was called by God into ministry and is an Ordained Reverend with the Assemblies of God.

Ryan holds a Master of Arts in Ministry Leadership with a concentration in Church Revitalization and has been in vocational ministry for over twenty years. He and his wife, Linaya, have three world-changing children: Bryce, Gavin, and Lilly.

Ryan is the Lead Pastor at Calvary Christian Assembly (the *Jesus Loves Seattle* church). Passionate prayer and worship music, encouraging Bible teaching, and generous community outreach serve as his ministry hallmarks. Pastor, community leader, Rotarian, music artist, and author, Rev. Ryan's sole purpose and mission is to encourage health, unleash hope, and inspire faith by helping people find and follow Jesus.

Connect more with Ryan and share your turnaround story. Write to ryanbunbury@gmail.com or text (916) 833-2773.